Royal Roosters and Chickens
Coloring Book

Artist designed and hand drawn
by Celeste Collings

Royal Roosters and Chickens

Artist and illustrator, Celeste Collings is known for creating art that touches the heart in everyone! Her love of mixed media and unique design style blend to create fun designs for hours of enjoyable and relaxing coloring!

She is listed in private and corporate collections as well as showing her fine art in over 30 national and international exhibitions.

For more information please visit us
www.royalchickens.com

ISBN-13:978-1541281943
ISBN-10:1541281942

Royal Roosters and Chickens

This book belongs to

_____

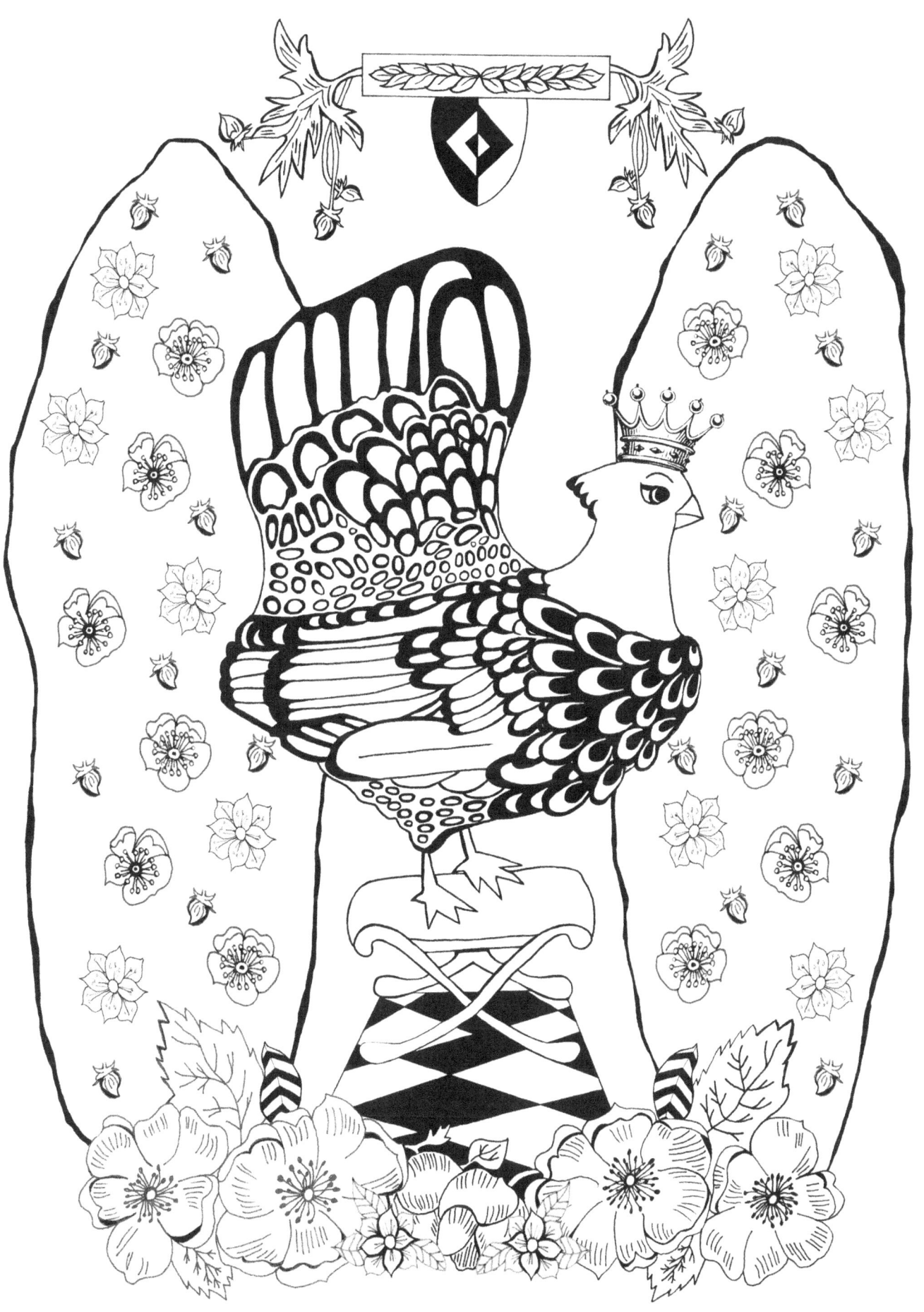

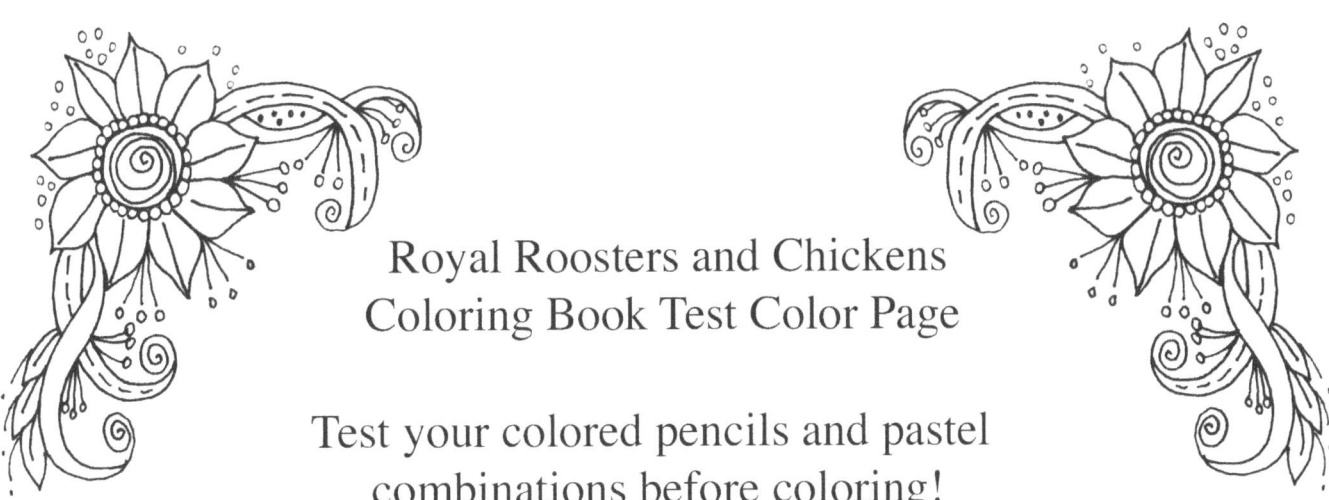

Royal Roosters and Chickens
Coloring Book Test Color Page

Test your colored pencils and pastel
combinations before coloring!

For best results put a blank paper
between pages when coloring with
markers to prevent bleed through.